Goldilocks and the Clever Plan

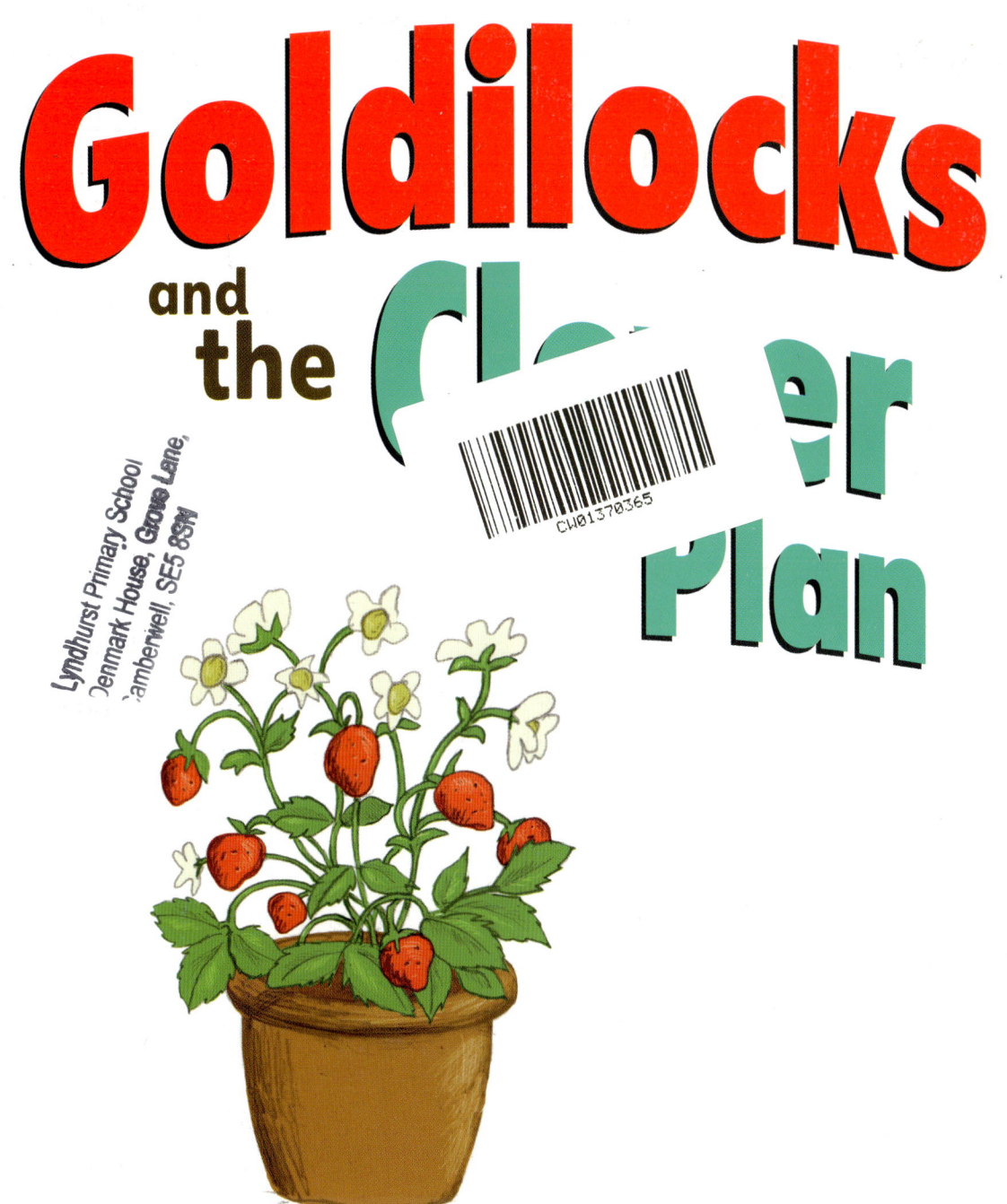

Written by Smriti Prasadam-Halls
Illustrated by Andy Rowland

For Gabe – S.P-H.

It was a sunny morning at the home of the three bears.

"Let's go for a walk!" said Mama Bear.

"Yes!" said Papa Bear. "But I hope no one visits while we are out. They may not be as friendly as Goldilocks."

The bears made a clever plan. "We'll set a trap!" they said.

Mama Bear tied a trip wire across the path.

"Hee hee!" she laughed. "If someone tries to come in, they will trip over this wire!"

She went off to fetch her scarf.

Papa Bear came out. He dug a big hole under the door mat and put a line of toy cars around it.

"Ha! If someone tries to come in, they will fall into this hole!" he chuckled.

He went off to fetch his hat.

Baby Bear got a pot of paint and put it on top of the door.

"If someone tries to come in, they will get a big surprise!" he giggled.

But! Oh dear! The bears had forgotten *one* small thing ... they had forgotten to tell each other their clever plans.

And so …
"Yuck!" yelled Mama Bear as she opened the door and got splashed with paint!

"Help!" cried Baby Bear as he tumbled over his toy cars and fell into the hole.

"Ouch!" shouted Papa Bear as he fell over the trip wire. He went right through the gate ... and into a puddle!

"I don't think our plan was very clever," said Baby Bear.

"Never mind!" chuckled Papa Bear. "Let's go for a walk anyway. *No one* will want to break into our house *now*!"

The bears enjoyed their walk in the woods. When they got home, they noticed a funny thing ... their house looked as good as new!

"Who's been cleaning my door?" asked Mama Bear.

"Who's been mending my gate?" gasped Papa Bear.

"Who's been picking up my cars?" cried Baby Bear.

And they ran in to see.

"Hello, everyone!" called Goldilocks.

The bears were very happy to see her. They were also very happy to see their tidy house. They told Goldilocks all about their not-so-clever plan!

"Let's all have a slice of cake," said Papa Bear.

"Now that really *is* a clever plan!" giggled Goldilocks.